The Right To Be Me

This book is dedicated to my three inspirations - Lara, Christopher and Andy.

Design and layout by Jan Vickers 2002
Illustrations by Kate Spurway

This book was originally commissioned by East Ayrshire Council and was influenced by the UN Convention on the Rights of the Child.

If you would like training materials or inservice on this book, please contact Mindstretchers.

ISBN 095448833 - 4

Mindstretchers Ltd
Glenruthven Mill
Abbey Road
Auchterarder
Perthshire
PH3 1DP
Scotland
U.K.

Telephone: +44(0)1764 664409
Fax: +44(0)1764 660728

E-mail: enquiries@mindstretchers.co.uk
Website: www.mindstretchers.co.uk

The Right To Be "Me"

Foreword

Celebrating our youngest citizens should be one of the most important parts of our day. To support and promote a young persons self awareness brings benefits for all.

A child's sense of themselves is how they begin to realise who they are and their place within their family and the community.

Claire has at the heart of her writing the needs of each child she comes into contact with. Each child is approached as a unique person who should be respected, and offered equal time, stimulation and love.

Her ideas are as always exciting, innovative and realistic. They will be a joy to participate in by both adult and child. I look forward to using these ideas and adopting the principles within my own practice and would encourage everyone using this book to enjoy it too.

Alice Sharp.

This book is for anyone who works with and cares for young children and who likes to reflect on how young children develop in a wide variety of environments.

It will hopefully encourage people to think and reflect a little about how we encourage children to feel good about themselves so that they feel confident to meet new challenges.

The emotional aspects of a child's development are influenced by everything around them both intangible and tangible. To define the importance of a smile or the subtlety of body language is a challenging task. In the process of creating this book the high quality of home, centre and educare provision across many countries has been examined.

We hope we have created a document that raises the importance of creating a sense of self in the young children in our care, before a more structured approach to learning is introduced. The document is not a curriculum to be followed, but a document to support reflection and thought. Many of the issues are connected to the atmosphere and ethos created by individual people as well as the Parents and Early Years Team. We hope that it will be read and enjoyed by anyone working or living with young children.

A great deal can be shown about the society of a country from the way that it treats the youngest children in its care. There are two main areas of early years provision that have influenced the thinking about the development of an early years curriculum with a focus towards nurturing the inner self and the positive self esteem that it creates.

♦ The Danish Child Welfare Commission (1981) states that they aim to give children a central position in the life of grown ups. The culture and social expectation in many of the Scandinavian countries support this through very practical actions such as paternity leave, leave of absence to care for sick children, even down to closure of meetings to enable parents to attend nursery events.

♦ Te Whariki is the name of the Early Childhood Curriculum in New Zealand. It symbolizes a woven mat, which integrates Maori culture and principles with the existing curriculum to create a 'bi-cultural curriculum'.

It has five goals, which are: -

Well being (the health and well being of the child is protected and nurtured)

Belonging (children and their families feel a sense of belonging)

Contribution (opportunities for learning are equitable and each child's contribution is valued)

Communication (the language and symbols of their own and other cultures are promoted and protected)

Exploration (the child learns through active exploration of the environment)

The integrated nature of Te Whariki has been popular in Scotland and many of the new curriculum documents are linked to it. One of the important aspects of it for this document is the emphasis on an underlying sense of well being.

The design of our book is linked to the philosophy that children have the right to high quality care/education. There is a wide variety in the quality and type of experience that young children in our society encounter. The rights that we have endorsed are those that we feel are central to the development of a sense of self. They are outlined below. Children learn in a holistic way, with everything connected. The rights that we mention are fundamental to the child and cross over all aspects of a curriculum through the early years and on into life.

The pages include statements made from a child's perspective (Italics) and the main text written from the perspective of the adult. The ideas presented through the illustrations are developed more fully on the black and white pages of the book to support practice in a variety of settings.

The Rights Of The Child

The right to be part of a group

Let me be an individual with a name, with my own ideas and thoughts but also help me to feel that I belong to a larger group.
Talk to the other adults who help me learn so that you all work together to help me.
Help all the adults I play with to be aware of how important they are to me, because they affect the way I am.

The right to be cared for

Try to help me grow in any way you can.
Help me to feel that I am cherished, but let me make some choices.
Let me relax, sleep and play every day.
Help me to eat and drink well so that my body will grow.

The right to be treated with respect

I need you to help me to feel that I am special in the world.
Think about the way you treat me, I am an individual with my own rights.

The right to a sense of wellbeing

Give me the chance to feel good about myself so that I develop in a harmonious way.
See my achievements and let me know how well I am doing.
Help me to feel O.K, even when my life is unsettled.

The right to have someone to communicate with

Make me important in your life so that you understand my body language.
Allow me to tell you what I am thinking and feeling.
Listen to me and try to understand my thoughts.
Give me the time so that I can show/tell you about my discoveries.

The right to have time to learn

Allow me to learn in places that help me to feel secure.
Let me be flexible in the way I learn; encourage my love of learning.
Give me time to develop my ideas.
Try not to limit my potential through your expectations.

The right to be encouraged to use sensory learning

Watch me play and then provide me with things to play with that develop all my senses.
Talk to each other about the way I learn so that you know me.

The right to move

Support me by giving me the freedom and space to move inside and outside.
Provide me with the activity and mobility that I need and enjoy.
Encourage me to learn to move, so that I can find out more about the place I am in.

The right to explore and discover

Encourage me to try.
Give me the chance to find out what the world is all about with you near by.
Let me move out into the world when I show that I am ready to take the step.

The right to be in a safe environment

Watch over me and keep me safe from harm.
Support me when I face a challenge, but don't over protect me.
Reassure me, so that I feel I can challenge myself.

The Rights Of The Child

The right to be

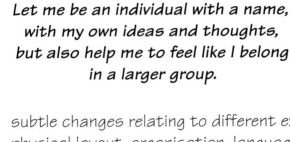

Let me be an individual with a name, with my own ideas and thoughts, but also help me to feel like I belong in a larger group.

Children move between groups of people who care for them. We encourage them to enter these groups either through choice or through a lack of integrated care settings to meet family needs. The group may be family members, a childminder, a playgroup, a nursery, a centre, a creche. Some children learn to move between all these groups with the ability to understand subtle changes relating to different expectations such as behaviour, physical layout, organisation, language, and resources. In order to feel an inner confidence to enter these groups, children need to be aware of themselves as individuals.

We can support children through these transitions by providing continuity and explanations. As a parent/carer we are the continuity, we can try to explain the reasons why people behave in different ways, why a child can put glue on with a brush in one place and not use it at all in another. As adults we are able to communicate with all the people who care for a child so that individual children know where they are, what is expected of them. A real partnership has to be willing on both sides. The communication should be about achievements but also to discuss challenges and solutions so that all carers have a sense of ownership and involvement.

part of a group

Young children are often in a situation over which they have no control. A feeling of loss of control can create feelings of uncertainty about their sense of themselves as valuable people. We can encourage children to overcome this by involving them in some of the decisions such as where to store the bricks, which cup to use for the juice, or what they would like to do.

Talk to other adults that help me learn so that you all work together to help me.

We live in a wider group in our communities.

Help all the adults I play with to be aware of how important they are to me, because they affect the way I am.

All people a child comes into contact with will give them a feeling of how important they are. The way people treat us gives us a sense of who we are and how much respect we have. If we treat children in a respectful way they will develop respect for themselves and then in turn be able to respect other people.

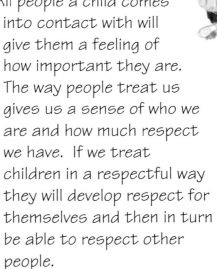

The right to be

Suggested resources and opportunities

People who make frequent use of the child's name, pronounce it properly and learn how to spell it.

People who ask after a child's family and friends.

People who are aware of the effect they have on children's mood and emotion.

People who are from the wider community such as shopkeepers, police, local artists.

Use of specific praise from all the people who work with the child.

Talking and Thinking Books that record children's ideas/observations so that planning starts with a child's interests (large floorbooks that raise the profile of talking and thinking).

Responsibility within the group to encourage children to care for it such as small brooms, tools to tend the garden, hand held vacuum.

Spaces that allow children to be alone, such as individual floor mats, small dens.

Flexible plans that encourage children to explore a variety of social groupings, in a variety of locations, such as pairs at a table, large groups in the sand outside, small groups around the pebble tray, an individual on the floor.

Prams and chairs that face each other rather than in a row.

Coat peg with a photograph of the child in various settings such as family, nursery, childminder.

part of a group

Photographs of the child mounted alongside their work to celebrate the effort and process not the end product.

Familiar objects/sounds from their cultural environment e.g. language, music, fabrics.

Seating/welcome area that takes into account the people coming in e.g. space for prams.

Parents notice board that is regularly updated.

Newsletters that involve children through; pictures, words they have said, ideas that they have.

Photo-books to record activities during the day for parents to share with the child.

Profiles/Records that include spaces for parent/carer comment and information and children's reflections on their learning.

Tape of the child talking at the centre for parents to take home to listen to.

Inclusion of wider group of people such as siblings, grandparents.

Link projects where appropriate, that explore emotional aspects of child development.

A place where a child's family is welcome and their opinion is valued such as parents room, social events that suit the parents involved, joint record keeping.

The right to

Try to help me grow in any way you can.

To enable a child to feel cherished there are times when a child's needs should be put first. Children can be faced with a view of themselves that makes them feel that they are not 'good enough' to meet adult expectations. We should see children as special personalities who need to be given choices within a supportive environment.

Children depend on us to give them the opportunity to play, balanced with quieter times to rest and relax.

We should observe the children in our care and learn their patterns so that their individual needs can be met by the caring adults around them.

We should listen to the children in our care and come to know the wider group they belong to. Children do form attachments or connections to adults who care for them. Every child and the family it is attached to will have different needs and ways of caring for their child. We should try to accept the rich variety of parents and carers.

Help me to feel that I am cherished, but let me make some choices.

be cared for

When practitioners, parents and carers work together, their strengths will help a child grow socially, emotionally, physically and intellectually.

Young children are affected by their physical needs. They will show us through various ways such as their behaviour, expression, and gesture.

Let me relax, sleep and play actively every day.

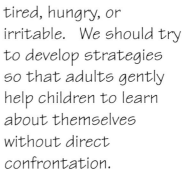

We should support children so that they can start to understand their body's demands. A young child will find it hard to accept an adult telling them that they are tired, hungry, or irritable. We should try to develop strategies so that adults gently help children to learn about themselves without direct confrontation.

Help me to eat and drink well so that my body will grow.

The right to

Suggested resources and opportunities

People who respond to children's needs with warmth and affection.

People who support them in learning how to care for themselves e.g. cleaning their shoes, washing their hands, feeding themselves.

People who show how 'they' care by considering other people and their likes and dislikes.

People who provide a sense of 'nearness' e.g. being near the sleeping area, to watch over the children as they sleep.

Bean bags/soft cushions to sleep on.

Colour coded linen to change for each child.

Resources that are the correct size for their body e.g. small brooms, brushes, tables, chairs etc.

Tape recorder with soft music to go to sleep.

Routines to settle children off to sleep/relax.

Soft lighting and secluded areas to explore.

Gentle calm background colours that create a peaceful environment.

Tape recording of the parent's voice.

Comforting objects left by the parent/carer.

be cared for

Photographs of the children's special people beside their bed/resting area.

A place to put their own special things e.g. bag.

Interesting objects to explore such as mirrors, mobiles, boxes, bags.

Familiar furnishings etc. such as sofas, curtains etc. to create a cozy atmosphere.

Healthy food to eat through the day.

Storage of food/milk in the fridge that is well labelled.

Area for breast-feeding mothers.

Self help area with a choice of food attractively displayed.

Low chairs around a table to include babies so that they are part of the social occasion of eating.

Healthy food and drinks e.g. water/milk.

Healthy routines such as cleaning teeth, washing hands.

Opportunity to talk about their emotions and feelings.

Opportunity to care for other people/animals (younger siblings, pets, adults, people in the community).

Opportunity to play in 'family groups'.

The right to be

*I need you to help me feel that I am
special in the world.*

Children are the smallest members of our society, most important and they deserve to have our respect. Our children will pick up messages about how important they are from a very early age. Eye contact, closeness, having a sense of belonging somewhere, time to talk and listen is all-important to a young child. The small details about the way that people behave all give subtle messages to young children about how special they are.

When we show that we respect children they can begin to understand what it is to be an individual. Through time, self-respect and a belief in themselves can develop and will become part of a child's emotional intelligence that will enable them to learn more effectively. When a child feels that they have a secure place and a status they are in turn, more likely to treat others with respect and care.

treated with respect

Respect for children extends to their possessions and people they care about, since a young child sees them as extensions of themselves. We should consider some of the hidden messages we send to children for example when we put a favoured toy in an old box on a high shelf. We need to think about the underlying messages that we give to young children.

Think about the way you treat me,
I am an individual with my own rights.

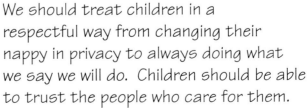

When we communicate with young children we should note that they are individuals and they have a right to be spoken to in a gentle way, not to be bullied. If we ask questions that ask for a choice such as "shall we tidy up?" young children have the right to say no!

We should treat children in a respectful way from changing their nappy in privacy to always doing what we say we will do. Children should be able to trust the people who care for them.

The right to be

Suggested resources and opportunities

People who understand a child's right to say no.

People who make eye contact when they speak.

People who concentrate and think when children are communicating with them.

People who involve children in conversations.

People who encourage children to say hello and goodbye to their friends and visitors.

People who ask a child how they are, and remember important events.

People who speak in a quiet way and work alongside children.

People who think about the different ways that children learn, so that a range of approaches are used.

People who consider children's motivation and interest when they plan.

People who do what they say they will do.

Resources that are open ended to enable children to use them in their own way, such as boxes, scarves, corks.

treated with respect

Resources that are familiar to the child from their cultural background such as types of food, clothing and music.

Resources that offer something special to a child's experience e.g. an interesting object from the carers home.

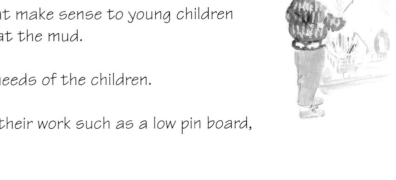

A place where details matter such as the neatness of displays, body language of the adults, warm welcoming areas.
Photographs of the child, family and friends in a place that the child can reach and see as often as they want.

A place to put their important things such as a pebble, teddy or comforter.

A place that shows you value the objects such as a bookshelf/Perspex fronted cupboard rather than an old box.

Opportunities to make individual creations.

Plans that are a blend of child initiated and adult created learning opportunities.

Plans that use contextual learning that make sense to young children such as going to the shops or looking at the mud.

Flexible timetables to respond to the needs of the children.

Space at a child's height to celebrate their work such as a low pin board, easy fix rail.

The right to a

Give me the chance to feel good about myself so that I develop in a harmonious way

We encourage children to do a great many things in their lives, to push themselves, to take small risks so that each day they develop their skills or gain new knowledge. Do we place as much effort into giving children the opportunity to **feel good** about themselves? If children are to be at the centre of our society then we need to develop the ability to put aside other pressures to say great things to them.

Children use the people around them to gain a sense of themselves. We need to give children clear, consistent positive feedback about how they are doing. Specific comments are more effective because they allow children to understand exactly what they have done that was positive. Not knowing what you are to do or how to do it can create a feeling of uncertainty.

Help me to feel O.K. even when my life is unsettled.

sense of wellbeing

We would be achieving great things, if at the end of the day we had said a positive thing to each child that we had met.

We will meet children who may be going through an unsettled time for all different kinds of reasons. In an ideal world

See my achievements and let me know how well I am doing

all children would go through a lifetime which although challenging, still has a sense of stability. We can offer stability for a child, by being there in a consistent way, by listening and supporting, often without verbal comment.

Children 'sense' situations and atmospheres. They respond to the environment, events and people around them. Not just to the words they say but to unspoken messages, conveyed through facial expression, body language, tone of voice etc. The way that they show that they have 'sensed' something varies with every child.

The right to a

Suggested resources and opportunities

People who want to be with young children.

People who take time to look attentively at the child when they are talking, and maintain positive eye contact.

Consistent people who give clear feedback to the child and explain the reason.

People who remember the special things about a child, the birthdays, favourite foods, or a cup, the names of a family.

People who give children choice and responsibility throughout the day, such as which table cloth to put onto the table, or when they go outside and for how long.

People who give specific praise such as "Well done Chris because..you put your coat on".

People who appreciate that confidence develops through the experience of experimentation and failure.

Materials that allow chidlren to see themselves e.g. mirrors thatare hand held, on the floor, in a tunnel, on the wall. Mirrors that change the shape of their image such as flexible sheets.

Resources that can be used by all children with a range of mobilities,

Large, low trays on the floor to crawl into for sand, leaves, rolling objects, tinsel.

sense of wellbeing

Food area where young children sit at the same table as the older ones/adults.

Resources that help children to feel valued such as tables that are covered with attractive wipe clean tablecloths, to create a positive feeling about mealtimes. Objects in the centre of the table to talk about.

Adult and child working together to master new skills such as using a spoon to support the child starting to self feed.

Food presented in a positive way e.g. a choice of child sized portions that are attractively presented.

Resources that support self help skills such as lidded jugs and cups that encourage children to develop life skills.

Appropriate routines to give stability to children, for example getting the table ready at lunchtimes. welcome songs, a special place to put personal objects/comforters.

Routines that take each individual into account such as sleeping time.

Auditory stimulation and comfort from tapes of parents/carers talking and singing. Tapes of familiar household noises.

Comforters and a special place for them to go when the child is ready to put them aside.

Objects from home such as a favourite cup, or perhaps a parents jumper for a baby to smell.

The right

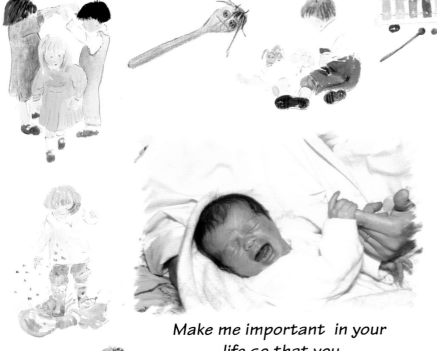

Make me important in your life so that you understand my body language

We all communicate. All of us use body language, tone of voice, gestures, writing and marks, pictures, and diagrams in different ways.

Children tell us a great deal through their nonverbal communication. People who work with young children need time to develop the skills to read the body movements of a baby, or the inventive language of a 2-year-old.

We communicate when there is another person to contact. The communication can take place between a group of babies, toddlers or young child. The desire young children have to be close to other people and to see their face demonstrates how important these simple actions are to them.

Children learn how to communicate by hearing and watching people around them. Whilst being pushed in a buggy or sitting at a table to eat, social interaction occurs when we join a group of any type. Time should be given for babies to play alongside more developed children, so that children can tune into each other's communication patterns more effectively. Younger children are encouraged to communicate when they want to make brief excursions to move from their peer group to see older siblings and friends, and communicate when they wish to return to their home base.

Listen to me and try to understand my thoughts.

to communicate

People respond to a flexible approach to learning where children learn and develop at different rates. Children should be encouraged to talk to us and we should therefore give ourselves the time to listen, we encourage children to discover and explore, so we should make the time to share in their wonderment. Children are able to think and reflect at a very early age, and we should be there to take the responsibility of understanding their way of communicating it to us.

We encourage children to communicate by giving them clear opportunities that require them to use

Allow me to tell you what I am thinking and feeling.

their skills to pass on information. We should recognise our children's exploration of the written and spoken word in a positive way. We respond as human beings if we know that we have people around us who value us enough to actively listen, engaging the heart, mind and body.

Give me the time so that I can show and tell you about my discoveries.

The right

Suggested resources/opportunities

People who watch children to find out their needs and preferences.

People who value the importance of body language, voice tones and facial expressions.

People who recognize that children communicate from the moment of birth.

Members of the staff team who work as key workers to the child and the family.

A familiar adult who will stay with the child throughout the time in the centre to develop consistent links with the child and the home.

Key workers are given time to link to families before the children start.

Adults share with one another the appropriate information to help identify children's individual ways of communicating their needs.

Adults and children who play together on the floor.

Children are given time to communicate through picture symbols for personal objects/people, spoken language and physical gestures.

to communicate

Places that have quiet, cozy areas away from distraction to enable child/child or child/adult interaction.

Individual, paired and small group opportunities for communication for all children.

Resources that encourage talking and listening such as telephones, listening centres, music, noisy toys, storytelling.

Resources that encourage mark making such as paper, forms, and envelopes.

Toys that can represent people/things such as puppets, cardboard boxes.

Flexible use of time, space and resources to respond to rates and styles of communication.

Books of all shapes and sizes placed on a low bookshelf for easy access.

The right to have

Allow me to learn in places that help me to feel secure

Children's learning is connected to their emotions. They find learning more challenging when they are spending a large portion of their time controlling extremes of emotion, or have no motivation or interest in learning.

Many children are able to experience a huge range of emotions in a short space of time. A toddlers brain and body are in the process of trying to explore where they belong in the world and where the boundaries lie. We can support them in the development of their emotional literacy, which is the ability to talk about how you feel so that other people can empathise with you. We need to acknowledge emotions in young children, so that they feel they have the right to feel and experience them. Our role is to offer a nurturing environment to help

Let me be flexible in the way I learn, encourage my love of learning

time to learn

children express their feelings and emotions. If a child is secure within, then the effect of these extremes of emotion will not have a lasting effect. We can offer security through routines, familiar places and faces, home based environments that use language spoken at home, and familiar household items.

Give me time to develop my ideas.

All people have the ability to achieve their full potential if they are given the opportunity. We can support children by not limiting their potential with our own pre-conceived ideas. We should try to avoid set expectations for children at certain ages, instead we should motivate all the children by taking them forward at their own pace.

Carers should create a high quality environment so that each child is affected in the most positive way.

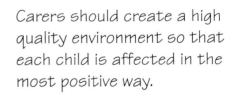

Try not to limit my potential through your expectations

The right to have

Suggested resources and opportunities

People who can see the wonder and excitement of the world from a young child's perspective.

People who are positive and motivated to be with children.

Provision of accessible outdoor and indoor learning areas.

Equipment that is clearly organised, at a level that children can access

Space to move freely.

Enclosed areas to settle.

Home style rooms with familiar furniture such as sofas, bookcases, bean bags for adults and children to snuggle into.

Gentle lighting and soothing colours in resting areas.

A rich environment with posters, pictures, words and photographs.

Objects to touch and explore in low level display boxes.

Smooth lines and curving partitions.

Furniture that supports learning such as large, shallow trays to keep equipment near by the baby.

time to learn

Experiences that are offered on the floor rather than at tables.

Home based learning experiences such as water play at a sink, real vegetables in the home corner, a laundry basket to sort and classify, real flowers to smell, mud to dig in.
Layout of a room that 'makes sense' such as play dough in the home corner.

Experiences that include repetition in an exciting way.

Resources and opportunities that respond to the way young children are motivated, such as filling and emptying, transporting and travelling, looking and finding.

Multisensory resources across all areas of learning.

Time to revisit resources and opportunities over a series of days to allow a depth of learning.

Children of different ages and stages playing together to learn from each other.

Times of discovery learning with little adult talk to enable the child to explore materials without distraction.

Materials that can be used during play in a variety of ways, free from an adult design such as boxes, fabric, blocks, tubes.

Stimulating, interesting places for babies to be.

The right to be encouraged

Watch me play and then provide me with things to play with that develop all my senses.

Our brains are created in such a way that we gather information through our ability to move to interact with environments and touch, smell, hear, taste and look around us. A baby's brain has all the brain cells that it will ever have, it does however become more refined in the way that they are used. Our brains are all different and we have a preferred way of learning partly linked to our senses. The way we feel about ourselves as learners can affect the amount we achieve. It is essential to encourage children to develop a positive attitude to learning throughout their life.

It is important to be aware that people learn in different ways. One child may be very ordered and precise, whilst another may learn in a creative, random way.

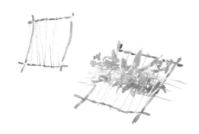

to use sensory learning

If we look at children when they are engaged in learning, we will be able to see traits or preferences developing. If we respond to these by the way that we present resources, ask questions and organise opportunities we will be encouraging children to be self-motivated and eager to learn because the process engages and sustains them.

Children learn through their senses. Some commercial plastic toys are too focused on the sense of sight. Simple, natural resources that feel rough, real lemons that smell and taste unusual, short lengths of chain that make sounds when they are dropped down a tube, stones that have a cold touch will all excite young children. Open-ended objects such as bricks, boxes,

Talk together about the way I learn so that you know me.

and material are full of possibilities to engage children's imaginative skills for a longer period of time than an adult designed house.

The right to be encouraged

Suggested resources and opportunities

People who recognise the different ways children learn.
Opportunities to link sensorial learning across all environments can be achieved through baby books, photo diaries and sensory toys and equipment in home/school bags.

Sight

Mirror ball and torch.
Games of hide and seek and peepo.
Black and white pattern on fabric/flooring/toys.
Bag of fabrics that are visually dissimilar.
Photographs of family and friends.
Containers that hide objects such as Wellington boots, boxes, bags.
People who make eye contact with children.
Coloured /moving lights on the walls, windows, ceiling, white umbrella.

Touch

Range of textured clothes/fabric in a basket with objects to hide.
Floor surfaces with a variety of textures.
Baskets of objects to reach out to touch e.g. loofa, stone, wooden bowl, napkin ring, pom-pom, glittering purse, lemon.
Sensory Boards (A4 sized wooden boards or larger with objects stuck to them such as corks, carpet, chain lengths, kitchen scrubbers, off-cuts of wood, sandpaper, pan lid).
People, who join in to hold, tickle and cuddle children.
Tactile objects in the bath/water tray such as flannels, spaghetti, jelly.
Fans, paper or electric to create a breeze.

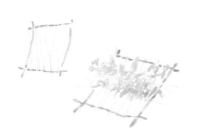

to use sensory learning

Sound

Natural materials that make a sound such as dry leaves, wood blocks, stones, or twigs.

Containers to collect them in such as metal buckets (variety of shapes and sizes), wooden bowls, plastic tubs.

Objects that make a sound such as horn, rattle, tins of dried food stuffs, scrunchy paper.

Loud clocks to hide and find.

Songs, rhymes and all types of music.

Smell

Perfume sprayed on fabric squares/natural products such as wooden rings and wicker hoops.

Smelly bags e.g. Lavender/herb/teaground coffee/spices (made from washing tablet bags or old clean socks).

Flowers with a scent.

Pot Pourri.

Taste

Provide specific areas/boxes of objects to mouth.

Provide a variety of tastes and experiences within the centre.

Heuristic play bags

Treasure baskets (Goldschmied 1994)

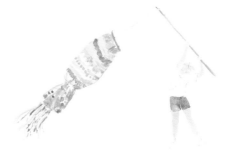

The right

*Provide me with the
activity and mobility
that I need and enjoy.*

Children learn so much through movement. If we look at a child from birth, their understanding of the world and their place within it is linked to their desire to move. Through the mastery of their body children develop an inner confidence and connections within the brain that has an effect on the way they learn. Many of the physical experiences that children naturally encounter such as crawling, climbing, skipping are important for brain development.

We need to provide an atmosphere and resources that positively encourage children to experience all kinds of movement such as their own bodies movement or visual movement when they watch objects turn and move.

*Support me by giving me the
freedom and space to move
inside and outside.*

to move

The outside environment offers young children space and freedom to move and experience the world around them. Through leaves on the ground to wind chimes hanging in the trees the environment is full of natural opportunities and should be explored to the full.
We need to give each child time to develop control of their body. These experiences such as sitting, reaching and rolling should be encouraged and celebrated for achievements in themselves.

We encourage children to move by providing them with small challenges. To achieve this we provide an interesting object to reach out to grasp, a box to open or the desire to climb a frame. When we watch young children we should be able to see them taking small risks to push themselves forward so that they can eventually explore the environments they live in and play in.

Encourage me to learn to move,
so that I can find out more about the
place I am in.

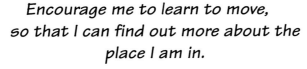

The right

Suggested resources and opportunities

People who are positive about moving and join in with the children to rock, sway, run and climb.

People that present the curriculum in an active way.

Natural and plastic hoops/rings in a variety of sizes.

Bells on ribbons to attach to the rings.

Ribbons of different weights, colours, textures and lengths to attach to a dolly peg/ring.

Small beanbags made from different fabrics, filled with a variety of materials to give a sense of weight.

Neck ties stuffed with toy stuffing to provide a variety of textured tubes.

Variety of boxes covered in bold patterns and textures to encourage children to open and close them.

Containers, such as small bags, to carry objects in.

Resources that encourage transporting such as Push along toys with hiding places, pull along carts.

Animals with collars and leads, to encourage journeying.

to move

Outdoor space with grass and hard surfaces, complete with slopes and different levels.

Bird table near the window.

Warm, waterproof outdoor clothing. Sunhats and shades so that children can move around freely outside.

Old containers/utensils to use outside to make pies.

Resources to watch movement/encourage physical movement such as kites, wind chimes, ribbons and bubbles, windmills, bubble tubes.

Physical equipment such as bats & balls in a variety of textures and sizes.

Bikes/trikes/trucks/prams.

Open ended materials to use in a variety of ways such as a cardboard box den, fabric river.

Objects that can be climbed on such as cushions, blocks.

Stable furniture to reach up to, climb on, crawl through.

Resources of all different sizes to grasp, and handle such as pegs, bean bags, socks, pom-poms.

Sounds and music to encourage children to move both indoors and out.

The right to explore

Encourage me to try.

To develop self confidence children need to learn it is alright to make mistakes. Some very young children develop a sense of fear of failure when they are learning. The desire to do it right, to make it perfect can be seen from children as young as two. Some children are so concerned about making mistakes that they do not attempt tasks. We should encourage children to spend time to test and try, to persevere so that this becomes part of the way they learn.

Give me the chance to find out what the world is all about with you near by.

We can give children too much structure and adult direction because we ourselves are bored with the opportunity! Children who are meeting glue for the first time may well spend many sessions dribbling and dropping it with no desire to stick objects together. They need time to do this so that they can explore the potential of the resource for as long as they wish.

and discover

As we play with them we can develop an understanding of the types of opportunity that motivate young children (ref. to the planning sheets at the back of the book). Such as the wonder they have at textures, colours, movement, smells, sounds in both the natural world and environments that adults create: Their fascination for living creatures: The thrill of physical movements such as filling and emptying, hiding and finding, transporting and travelling or sorting are common to all areas of play.

Let me move out into the world when I show you that I am ready to take that step

We offer support by being physically near to young children, so that in moments of uncertainty the child can look up and receive a positive boost from a smile or a nod. Although we ensure that they have a balanced range of experiences, we should give them time to think and talk, and give ourselves time to listen and respond to how much they already know and how much they still want to find out.

The right to explore

Suggested resources and opportunities

People that give children the opportunity to follow their interest.

People nearby to lend a hand, give praise and encourage in an atmosphere that gives children freedom to explore.

People who appreciate that making mistakes is part of the learning process.

People who encourage children to question and reflect e.g. What do you think ?   How could we ?

Resources to encourage children to look, e.g. magnifying glass, bug box, camera, window squares.

Resources used to create dough and other mixtures.

Presenting resources in containers that encourage them to explore, e.g. pieces of paper in a box, pebbles in a bag, objcts in jelly.

Household objects that are interesting to explore such as a metal colander, sieve, wooden spoon, an old Hoover, a peg, an empty squeezy bottle.

Variety of dressing up fabrics that are open ended enought to suggest a variety of animal/people/jobs.

Containers to collect objects in.

and discover

Basket of resources to change the water such as glitter, food colouring, ice cubes, bottles that squirt, bottles to pump, tiny containers, variety of spoons, variety of whisks, baby bubbles.

Mirror to look in from a variety of angles, above, below, flexed.

Materials and cardboard boxes to make a place to be.

Pictorial recipe cards designed to give simple instructions combined with free exploration.

Opportunities for water play such as Ice cubes in a container in the bath, basin/shallow bath to explore water, watering cans, sponges, containers of different sizes, funnels, tubing.

Outdoor/indoor clothing that can get dirty.

Accessories such as bags, hats, gloves, beads.

Footwear that protects feet from the water/mud.

Materials to explore colour such as mixing paints, food colouring, cellophane.

Coloured light such as acetate on windows/roof panels so that it is both horizontal and vertical.

Natural materials to explore.

The right to be in

We look to provide environments that are secure, exciting and stimulating for all children combined with a place that keeps them safe from harm. One of the greatest challenges we face as people who are around young children is to balance this with giving them the opportunity to take small risks that enable them to learn. Young children will try to find out how far they can go, whether it is a boundary linked to behaviour, or a physical skill such as climbing.

Watch over me and keep me safe from harm

When to stand back and when to step in is a dilemma for everyone working/living with very young children. If we step in too early we can prevent the child from learning new skills and if we don't step in we risk children harming themselves. The perceived risk in any situation can be considered and measures put into place to reduce the risk of serious injury. The safety measures we put into place should be reasonable, so that they limit injury without creating a sterile, dull place to be, with little opportunity for play and learning.

A way to introduce a safety measure that can be flexible, aware and responsible is to play alongside children.

a safe environment

Support me when I face a challenge, but don't over protect me

To hold a hand when they jump over waves or to run together through the woods, will not only support children in their discoveries, but will also monitor the risks involved. People working/ living with young children should try to be aware of where the feelings of fear are coming from. Is it the child or the adult? When we say to children 'Mind... you will fall' does it give them confidence or suggest an action?

There needs to be a balance between care and adventure in the life of a child under 3.

Playing outside has a large part to play in the life of young children; it offers space, fresh air, free resources such as mud, and a sense of freedom that cannot be replicated. We can support this play through being positive about being outside. In order to feel positive we need to feel prepared and secure in the environment we take children into. (Ref. page on the right to explore).

Reassure me so that I feel that I can challenge myself

The right to be in

Suggested resources and opportunities

An adult with a guiding hand who knows when to give support, and when to stand back.

People who support children to push their personal boundaries to take small risks that lead to learning.

People who explain to children the reasons behind some of the boundaries that are set for them.

People who take care and pay attention to detail, and so create a safe environment.

A team who all work together to be responsible for the safety aspects within the centre.

People who view safety as everybody's responsibility from staff to children to parents.

Furnishings provided at a child's level.

Systems in place for tidying up spills/mess.

Low dividers to create areas of play to enable a child to play freely within a defined space with an adult nearby.

a safe environment

Clean and fresh resources such as new play dough, clean floor cushions.

Battery operated /low heat lights for the children to use.

Food prepared in an hygienic way and stored in the fridge until required.

Hygiene wipes to minimize cross contamination.

Clear and clean areas to ensure high hygiene standards for toileting and washing hands, clothes etc.

Protected space that can be opened up to enable children to move to play with older children/more challenge.

Gates and guards to define dangerous areas.

Tools and utensils that teach children how to handle objects safely.

An environment that provides objects and areas to explore physical skills such as climbing, jumping, catching so that children develop the skills to control their movements.

Appendices

Effective Communication

In order for centres to ensure a breadth and balance in the experiences they offer children, it is neccessary to record elements on planning outlines for relevant adults to share.

The following pages offer some support for the development of home link opportunities and a child centred planning approach that are entitled Developmentally Appropriate Plans or D.A.P's.

Home Links
Home experiences are at the core of a young child's world and should be valued through high quality communication such as diaries, entry forms and newsletters. The features of effective communication strategies have been identified in this section.

Planning
The areas of the D.A.P's have been selected because they are important elements in the life of young children. Children are motivated by opportunities and behaviours that cross over curriculum boundaries such as filling and emptying or transporting. It is important that these elements are included in plans, along with a small scale focus/ interest which has been identified through observation in order to meet children's needs.

Evaluation
Following on from the D.A.P.'s are the evaluation sheets. An integral part of work with children is review and evaluation. Self evaluation, observation and analysis of learning will enable groups to support young children in a variety of ways throughout their development.

As with all generalised sheets the suggestions given should create a framework for homes, centres and care facilities that can be modified to meet the needs of the group.

Indicators of Good Practice for Homelinks

Features of an environment that supports talk

- Private area to sit and talk.
- Availability of time to talk.
- Attractive and relaxing decor.
- Ethos that values parent/carer opinions.

Features of a newsletter

- Written in a way that is sensitive to the people reading it.
- Catchy titles, humourous cartoon.
- Handwriting font for easy reading.
- Reduced text to enable people to scan over content.
- Include a monthly calendar type grid for carers to put straight on the wall with information already marked on (often on reverse).
- Attractive images/photos/drawings to communicate in a variety of ways.
- Children's interests noted to encourage continuation at home.

Features of a diary

- Written in a way that is sensitive to the people reading it.
- Personalised and anecdotal.
- Written using positive and specific statements.
- Include photographs or drawings made by the child.
- Include individualised achievements.
- Dated.
- Easily available to parents/carers.
- Attractive

Indicators of Good Practice for 0 - 3 Planning

Features of layout of planning

- Written in a way that is sensitive to the people reading it.
- Clear format e.g. enough space for recording individualised achievements.
- Handwriting font for easy reading.
- Reduced text to enable people to scan over content.
- Dated.
- Easily understood by parents/carers.
- Attractive

Features of content of planning

- Focuses on repeatable patterns of behaviour i.e. motivational keys.
- Areas of learning are:
    - Communication - looking, talking, gesture, mark making, singing.
    - Sensory experience.
    - Movement - licking, twisting, grasping.
    - Exploration and discovery - inside and outside.
    - Creating a sense of self - independence, choice.
- Reflects children's interests from home to carer.
- Children's interests noted to encourage continuation at home.

Features of evaluation

- Specific individualised statements recorded on the evaluation 'Do & Review' sheet.
- Written using positive and specific statements.
- Evaluation of learning is specific covering the following:
    - Review of provision provided - Adult interaction, parental involvement.
    - Evaluation of children's learning.
    - Motivation key - learning styles.
    - Action for specific children - People resources, space, time.
    - Development points.

"Developmentally appropriate plan"

Exploration & Discovery

Note down what experiences/resources/opportunities are available to encourage children to explore their environment.

Consider all the different ways that babies, toddlers and young children can develop a sense of exploration both indoors and out of doors, such as:-
Talking and reflecting
Questioning
Handling and touching
Looking and listening
Trying and failing

Ref. Motivational key below.

Creating a sense of self

Note down what experiences/resources/opportunities are available to encourage children to feel good about themselves.

Consider all the different ways that babies, toddlers and young children can develop a sense of self, such as:-
Positive, specific feedback
Independence
Success/failure
Challenge
Choice

Period ending

Children involved

```
Child
initiated
focus
```

How should the sheets be used ?

Movement

Note down what experiences/resources/opportunities that are available to encourage children to move.
Will it be an experience to develop the knowledge of what movement is?, a skill such as gross/fine motor?, or an attitude towards moving?.

Consider all the different ways that babies, toddlers and young children use movement, such as:-
Crawling, rolling, twisting, grasping, pinching, licking, balancing, walking, jumping, hopping, chewing.

Communication

Consider all the different ways that babies and young children communicate, such as:-
Looking/facial expression
Talking/making sounds
Listening
Gestures
Body language
Writing/mark making
Reading/exploring print
Include their understanding of why we communicate e.g.
To tell people what they want
To listen to others

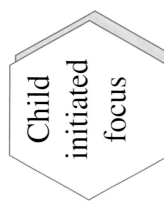

Sensory experiences

Note down what experiences/resources/opportunities that are available to encourage children to use their senses.

Consider all the different ways that babies, toddlers and young children approach all aspects of their learning through their senses, such as:-
Touch
Sight
Sound
Taste
Smell

Motivational key   Sorting/organising   Filling/emptying   Looking/finding   Transporting/carrying   Enclosing/enveloping   other

"Developmentally appropriate plan"

Period ending

Children involved

Child initiated focus

Example:-
Boxes and shiny objects

Exploration & Discovery

Provide a variety of different shaped boxes each containing one type of object such as pan scourers, metalic fabric, iridescent beetles, silver foil, wrapping paper

Adult interaction in the area to focus on handling and touching, sorting and reflective talk throughout e.g. "I wonder why … ?".

Creating a sense of self

Provide a variety of small boxes, blank for possible decoration with basket of heuristic materials/toys.

Adult interaction in the area to focus on personal favourites and choice of object to stick on box or to put inside. Emotional talk regarding preference, choice and similarities/differences within the group.

Communication

Provide three large cardboard boxes and mark making materials.
Adult interaction to focus on mark making as a method of communication.
Modelling of pencil grip and writing by staff.
Talking and listening relating to childrens interests e.g. moving around boxes, inside and outside, under and on top.

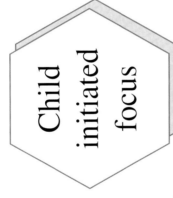

Sensory experiences

Provide five tactile boxes with
Touch - pieces of fabric
Sight - plastic mirrors, convex/concave
Sound - large bells presented in a variety of drawstring bags
Taste - teething rings, wooden/plastic
Smell - herb bags

Adult interaction to focus on the language of texture, sound etc.
Modelling of exploration and investigation by staff.

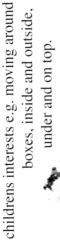

Movement

Provide a variety of large boxes with black/white and coloured patterns on the inside and outside.

Adult interaction in the area to focus on opening and closing boxes.
Extend into stacking enclosing objects within the boxes.

Motivational key

Filling/emptying
Sorting/organising

Transporting/carrying
Looking/finding

Enclosing/enveloping
other

47

"Developmentally appropriate plan"

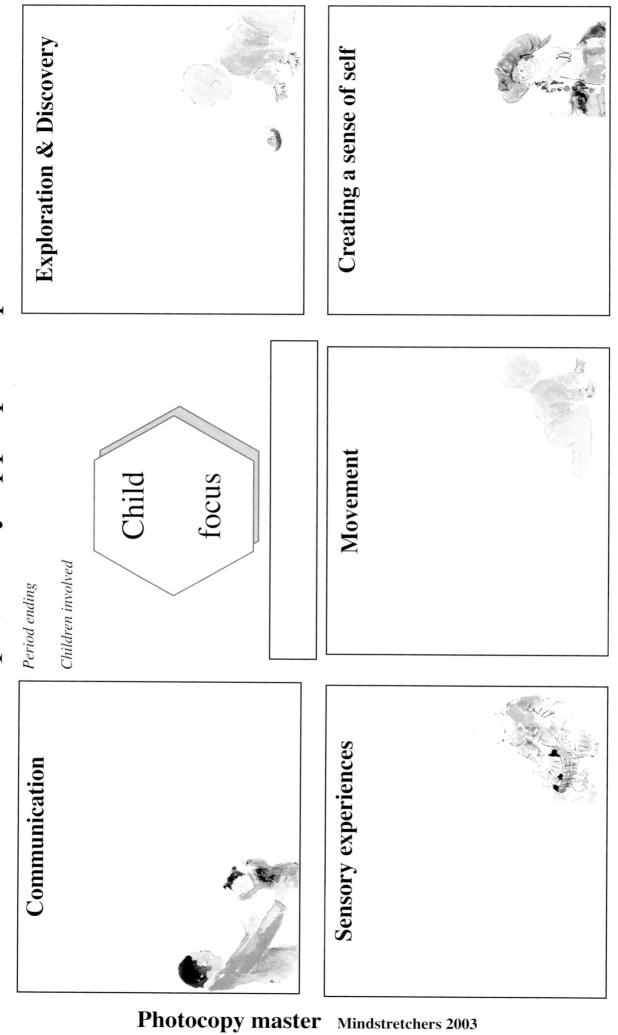

Exploration & Discovery

Creating a sense of self

Enclosing/enveloping
other

Period ending

Children involved

Child

focus

Movement

Transporting/carrying
Looking/finding

Communication

Sensory experiences

Filling/emptying
Sorting/organising

Motivational key

Evaluation sheet
0 - 3 years

Keyworkers

"Evaluation Sheet"

What is it for ?

Do
&
Review

What do we write about ?

Evaluation of childrens learning

Note down specific examples that show a change in a child's knowledge, skill, or attitude towards different areas of the planning sheet.

Did any children learn/develop something ?
If so, what ?
If not, why not ?

Development points

Note down what you are going to do next to keep the same lines developing so that the children's interest/ line of enquiry flows from day to day.

Ref: specific children

Staff signature
Management Signature

Motivation key/learning styles

Note down specific examples that show a change in a child's knowledge, skill or attitude towards learning and finding out.

Were there any examples of a child's preference developing ?
If so, what ?

What types of motivational keys are the children responding to ?

Review of provision provided

Adult interaction

What effect did the interaction have ?
Was it appropriate ?

Parental involvement

How did the other people in the child's environment improve the learning experience ?

Action for specific children

Note down specific support for individual children.

Consider:-
People - will you use your own skills to talk, listen, question, be nearby ?

Resources - Take them away ? Put more in ? Use them in a different way ? Organise/present them in a different form ?

Space - Make more ? Take some away ?

Motivational key   Filling/emptying
Sorting/organising

Transporting/carrying
Looking/finding

Enclosing/enveloping
other

49

"Evaluation Sheet"

Evaluation sheet
0 - 3 years

Period ending 22/10/02

Keyworkers
Jan and Linda

Children involved Phillip, Lara, Chris, Jo, Joshua & Elizabeth

Evaluation of childrens learning

Phillip picked up small pom pom in pincer grasp.

Lara seemed tired today and did not engage with the group. Very reliant on 'label comforter' today.

Chris said 'dink all gone' at the table.

Elizabeth at chrystal mobile at the window (pointed)

Development points

Re-introduce the exploration boxes - focus on the beetles to extend Joshua/Jo's interest.

Put down masking tape on floor with Chris to extend his interest in sorting/organising.

Staff signature
Management Signature

Do
&
Review

Example:-
Boxes and shiny objects

Review of provision provided

Adult interaction
Jo responded well to eye contact. Adult encouraged to bring him into the group. Elizabeth wandered around until supported by Linda. Seemed to respond to her physical location.

Parental involvement
Joanna's mum stayed to play today - really enjoyed storytelling.

Motivation key/learning styles

Chris motivated by lining up the boxes across floor and on edge of table. (Sorting/organising)

Elizabeth seems to have been attracted by light and movement of mobile.

Action for specific children

Elizabeth
People - Linda has made a connection so will continue to link to her.

Resources - introduce the glitter ball and torches in large boxes (den)/hologram paper in the boxes.

Time - Encourage Elizabeth to revisit large boxes and discovery boxes to find resources above.

Motivational key   Filling/emptying   Transporting/carrying   Enclosing/enveloping
                    Sorting/organising   Looking/finding   other

50

"Evaluation Sheet"

Evaluation sheet
0 - 3 years

Keyworkers

Period ending

Children involved

Evaluation of childrens learning

Development points

Review of provision provided

Do
&
Review

Motivation key/learning styles

Action for specific children

Staff signature
Management Signature

Enclosing/enveloping
other

Transporting/carrying
Looking/finding

Filling/emptying
Sorting/organising

Motivational key

Photocopy master **Mindstretchers 2003**

51

Bibliography and useful reading
Adult

Abbott, I. and Moylett, H. (1997) *Working with the under threes;* Responding to children's needs

Abbot, L./Nutbrown, C. (2001) *Experiencing Reggio Emilio* Open University Press

Alcott, Michael. (1997) *Introduction to Children with Special Educational Needs* Hodder and Stoughton

Beaver, Marion. (et al) (1995) *Babies and Young Children* Stanley Thornes (Publishing) Ltd.

Bilton, H. (1999) *Outdoor Play in the Early Years* David Fulton Publishers

Bredecamp, S.(1997) *Developmentally Appropriate Practice in Early Childhood Programmes* Washington NAEYC

Bruce, Tina. (1997) *Early Childhood Education* Hodder and Stoughton

Bruer.J. (1999) *The Myth of the First Three Years.* The Free Press

Cadwell, Louise Boyd. (1997) *Bringing Reggio Emilio Home* Teachers College Five Press

Castle, C.(2000) *For Every Child, the rights of the Child in words and pictures.* Unicef - Hutchison

Childs, Caroline. (2001) *Food and Nutrition in Early Years* Hodder and Stoughton

Clark, A/Moss, P. (2001) *Listening to Young Children The Mosaic Approach* National Childrens Bureau

David, Tricia. (1994) *Working Together For Young Children* Routledge Press

Donaldson, Margaret. (1987) *Childrens Mind's* Fontana Press

Dowling, M. (2000) *Young Childrens Personal, Social and Emotional Development* Paul Chapman Pub

Elliot, Lise. (1999) *Early Intelligence* Penguin Books

Fassani, Penny. (1999) *Early Years Care and Education S/NVQ Level 3* Heinemann

Fisher, J. (1996) *Starting from the Child* Open University Press

Goldschmied,E/Jackson,S. (1994) *People under Three* Routledge Press

Goldschmied, E/Jackson, S. (1994) *People Under Three (Young Children In Daycare)* Routledge Press

Graham, Philip/Hughes, Carol. (1995) *So Young, So Sad, So Listen* Gaskell

Hannaford. C. (1977) *The Dominance Factor* Great Ocean Publishers

Hobart, C/Frankel, J. (1999) *Childminding: A Guide to Good Practice* Nelson and Thornes

Hurst and Joseph. (1998) *Supporting Early learning,* The way Forward   Open University Press

Lindon, Jennie. (1993) *Child Development from Birth to Eight* National Childrens Union

Lindon, Jennie. (1998) *Child Protection and Early Years Work* Hodder and Stoughton

Milner, P./Birgit, C. Eds. (1999) *Time to Listen To Children* Routledge Press

Moyles, J. (1989) *Just Playing* Open University Press

Moyles, J. (1994) *The Excellence of Play* Open University Press

Mukherji, Penny. (2001) *Understanding Children Challenging Behaviour* Nelson Thornes Ltd.

Newcombe, Nora. (1996) *Child Development Change Over Time* Harper Collins College Publishers

New Zealand Ministry of Education (1993) *Te Whariki.* Wellington Learning Media Limited

OECD (2001) *Starting Strong* OECD

Pahl. K. (1999 *Transformations* Meaning Making in Nursery Trentham Books

Pascal, Christine/Bertram, Tony. (1997)*Effective Early Learning Case Studies* Paul Chapman Pub

Penn, Helen. (2000) *Early Childhood Services - theory, policy and practice* Open University Press

Roberts, R. (1995) *Self Esteem and Successful Early Learning.* London, Hodder and Stoughton

Rodd, J. (1998) *Leadership in Early Childhood* Open University Press

Scott (1996) in Nutbrown,C. (1996) *Children's Rights and Early Education*

Scottish Consumer Council (1989) *In Special Need* HMSO

SOEID (1999) *Curriculum framework for children 3-5* Edinburgh, The Scottish Office

Siraj-Blatchford, J. MacLeod-Brudenell,I. (1999) *Supporting Science, Design and Technology in the Early Years* Open University Press

Stallibrass, A. (1974) *The Self Respecting Child* Persens Publishing

UNICEF (2000) *For Every Child* Hutchison

Various (1995) *Sing Through The Day* The Plough Publishing House

Warden, C. (2001) *The Reflective Practitioner* Mindstretchers

East Ayrshire Publications:-

East Ayrshire Council (2000) *Planning for Early Learning* East Ayrshire Council

East Ayrshire Council (2000) *Fit Ayrshire Babies*

North Ayrshire Council (2001) *Fit Ayrshire Babies*

South Ayrshire Council (2001) *Fit Ayrshire Babies*

Child

Clark, Dorothy. (1999) *Grandpas Handkerchief* McDonald Young

Cousins, Lucy. (2001) *Maisies Favourite Animals* Walker

Cousins, Lucy. (2001) *Maisies FavouriteToys* Walker

Cousins, Lucy. (2001) *Maisies FavouriteClothes* Walker

Cousins, Lucy. (2001) *Maisies FavouriteThings* Walker

Cousins, Lucy. (2001) *Maisies Bedtime* Walker

Cousins, Lucy. (2001) *Maisie Dresses Up* Walker

Cousins, Lucy. (2001) *Maisies Bathtime* Walker

Hughes, Shirley. (2000) *Two Shoes New Shoes* Walker

Hughes, Shirley. (2000) *Bathwater's Hot* Walker

Hughes, Shirley. (2000) *When We Went to the Park* Walker

Larranage, Ana. (2000) *Family Farm* Treehouse

Larranage, Ana. (2000) *Playful Pets* Treehouse

Lobb, Janice. (2001) *Listen and See* Kingfisher

McBratney, Sam. (2002) *Guess How Much I Love You* Walker

Miller, Virginia. (2000) *On Your Potty* Walker

Miller, Virginia. (2000) *Get Into Bed* Walker

Miller, Virginia. (2002) *In a Minute* Walker

Nilsen, Hannah. (1998) *Lets Hang & Dangle* Zero to Ten

Oxenbury, Helen. (1995) *Dressing* Walker

Oxenbury, Helen. (1995) *Working* Walker

Oxenbury, Helen. (1995) *Playing* Walker

Oxenbury, Helen. (1995) *Friends* Walker

Oxenbury, Helen. (2000) *I Touch* Walker

Oxenbury, Helen. (2000) *I Hear* Walker

Oxenbury, Helen. (2000) *I Can* Walker

Parr, Todd. (2001) *This is My Hair* Walker

Parsons, Alexandra. (1996) *Being Me* Franklyn Watts

Parsons, Alexandra. (1996) *Your Special* Franklyn Watts

Rosen, Michael. (1996) *Poems for the Very Young* Kingfisher

Saunders, Pete/Myers, Steve. (1996) *Its My Life* Franklyn Watts

Sharrat, Nick. (2000) *Mum and Dad Make Me Laugh* Walker

Tofts, Hannah. (2002) *I Eat Veg* Zero to Ten

Tofts, Hannah. (2002) *I Eat Fruit* Zero to Ten